KILLING THE MURNION DOGS

KILLING THE
MURNION DOGS

For Peter —
. Thanks for listening!
Keep reading, keep writing!

Peace,

Joe Wilkins

[signature]

Norwich 2014

Black Lawrence Press

Black Lawrence Press
www.blacklawrence.com

Executive Editor: Diane Goettel
Book Design: Steven Seighman

Text copyright © 2011 Joe Wilkins

All rights reserved. Except for brief quotations in critical articles or re-
views, no part of this book may be reproduced in any manner without prior
written permission from the publisher:

Black Lawrence Press
326 Bigham Street
Pittsburgh, PA 15211

B. H. Fairchild, excerpt from "Speaking the Names" from The Art of the
Lathe. Copyright © 1998 by B. H. Fairchild. Reprinted with the permis-
sion of Alice James Books, www.alicejames.org.

"Atlantic City" by Bruce Springsteen. Copyright © 1982 Bruce Springsteen
(ASCAP). Reprinted by permission. International copyright secured. All
rights reserved.

Published 2011 by Black Lawrence Press, an imprint of Dzanc Books

ISBN-10: 0982876602
ISBN-13: 978-0982876602

First edition 2011

Printed in the United States

10 9 8 7 6 5 4 3 2 1

CONTENTS

Acknowledgments

Best New Poets 2006: "How to Bring Down Rain"

Boulevard: "Hallelujah, Somewhere, Steel"; "Meditation on the Treason of His Body"; "Ruins"

Boxcar Poetry Review: "Daybreak, Spokane, September 2001"; "A Dream of Home [Now it's dusk. . .]," "A Dream of Home [In defense . . .]," "Dream of Home [This time . . .]," "Dream of Home [For this . . .]," and "A Dream of Home [I wake . . .]" as "Five Dreams of Home"; "North Carolina by Greyhound: First Christmas after the Funeral"

The Briar Cliff Review: "A Roadside Diner in Iowa"

Burnside Review: "He Is Only Six and Has Not Yet Seen Anyone He Loves Die"

California Quarterly: "A New Trembling"

Crab Orchard Review: "Rain Ghazal"

Diner: "Letter to Liz from Houston"

diode: "The Big Dry, Montana, 1985"; "The Stone Eater"

Indiana Review: "Outside a Liquor Store in South Memphis"

Knockout: "The Bone Yard: A Phone Conversation with My Brother"; "Shooting Carp"; "Trying to Find Hollandale, Mississippi"

Linebreak: "Somewhere South of Miles City"

Northwest Review: "Bull Mountain Seasonal Bestiary"; "Killing the Murnion Dogs"

PANK: "Houston Sonnet"; "Mississippi Sonnet"

Silk Road: "Letter to Paul from Sunflower"

Slate: "The Names"

The Southern Review: "A Prayer"; "Highway"; "Jacketing"

Spoon River Poetry Review: "The Schoolteacher Blues Again"; "Body Theology"

Sweet: "Spiritual"

Swink: "The Land to the North"

Tar River Poetry: "Mississippi Delta"

Talking River Review: "The Log Works Near Midnight"

Touchstone: "Memphis Closes Her Eyes"

"Meditation on the Treason of His Body" was printed and distributed as a broadside by Broadsided Press. "North Carolina by Greyhound: First Christmas after the Funeral" was reprinted in

Best of Boxcar Poetry Review 2007. "Letter to Paul from Sunflower," "Mississippi Delta," and "Mississippi Sonnet" were reprinted in *The Southern Poetry Anthology II*: Mississippi. "Highway" was reprinted in *New Poets of the American West.* "Shooting Carp," "How to Bring Down Rain," "The Log Works Near Midnight," "The Land to the North," and "Letter to Paul from Sunflower" were reprinted at the online magazine *Escape Into Life.* "A Roadside Diner in Iowa" and "Memphis Closes Her Eyes" were reprinted on the Black Lawrence Press blog. Some of these poems also appeared in the limited-edition chapbook *Ragged Point Road* (Main Street Rag 2006).

Thanks to Lucas Howell, Steve Coughlin, and Paul Wilkins for reading countless drafts of these poems and offering substantial and wise guidance. And thanks as well to Robert Wrigley, Kim Barnes, and D. S. Butterworth for this world of words.

This is for Liz—everything for you.

How to Bring Down Rain

First, listen to the old men, watch
their dry lips flap. Throw sheep

bones in the river, ribs and unlinked
wings of spine. See the water wet them.

It's possible. Shoulder the sun
and walk the fence line west. Wipe

an oily head of sweat on your t-shirt.
Now come in for lunch—tomato

sandwich, ice water, the easy chair
in the cellar where you open all

your father's books, breathe their inky
dust. Then dream him an old man,

dream him dead again, years later,
when fathers should die. Chase your

sister with a broken mouse, tell your
brother lies about the neighbor girl.

Though there's no water anymore,
crack off the ram's skull, toss it

in the river too. See the gravel smooth
as skin, and your mother's face—

like gravel. Look at her. Know God
does not hate you, that nine years

of drought is child's play. Now come
back to the old men, see them rise

from wooden chairs, hear their bones
sift the dust of yesterday's rain.

Killing the Murnion Dogs

Everything dies, baby, that's a fact.
But maybe everything that dies someday comes back.

—Bruce Springsteen

A Dream of Home

Now it's dusk we haul boxes chairs
portraits framed in gray wood
people I have never known
a dead man shakes his head at us these twenty years
my mother kisses his grim mouth
takes the keys and drives
hell bent for the far highway
I say the gate's closed but she drives
faster wooden posts and wire and the truck's steel nose
slams through and out onto blacktop it's dark
maybe rain and before us
the whole world the whole world

Jacketing

Blood, he thinks,
        jerking the stillborn's hide
from its lifeless body, *is mother*
        of us all, and grabs
the bleating orphan, jackets
        this new skin across its back,
then turns to the dead lamb
        and with a jackknife opens
its throat—the bright, natal blood
        puddles in his palm—
and he splashes it over the nose
        of the skin-dressed surrogate,
and soil, he thinks, scooping a handful
        of shit and wiping it, too,
down the throat and chest, *our father.*

Now he rises and gently lifts
        the befouled, reborn imposter
into the pen with the lambless ewe
        and watches as they both sniff
and lick, and when finally
        she bumps the orphan
to her teat, he turns and leaves the shed—
        a low rim of light slips
over the eastern hills, a skein of ice
        still on the trough. *In ten days,*
he tells himself, *I'll cut away*
        the false skin, and he lifts his hands
before him where they steam with blood
        and shit. *Come September,*
I'll sell that lamb for slaughter.

Outside a Liquor Store in South Memphis

To make a meal
of moths,

                of mayflies—
black rag
of bat

          flaps in and out
of a streetlight's
incandescent stammer.

The dumb

     moon roped
and hung from eave
after rusted eave

              of the empty
warehouses north of Raines.

And this neon

         sermon
of blue Camels, High Life,
Thunderbird—

                  such bright
appetites in the city's itching dark.

Rain Ghazal

We drive south out of Memphis, dark shoulders of rain
behind us. Now we turn west, towards the river, into rain.

The setting sun tumbles like a drunk through the trees.
An old man fishing the bank lifts his face to sun-red rain.

I sit on the porch, sip whiskey from a jam jar, listen
for tree frogs and cicadas, for the lick of wind through rain.

Church Street is flooded. Don't try to drive it—it'll knock
your spark out. Road of dirty water, outrage of rain.

It comes down like rusty buckets, stumps, bricks. Each morning
she lifts herself from the dark water of dreams, but still it rains.

Wind shakes pecans from the dark trees. Before dawn
we wake and gather them in the fog, a gray wool of rain.

The soybeans drowned. The wheat rotted at the roots.
But green stalks swell between the dikes—rice loves rain.

A man holds a sopping bag over his head. Near the bayou,
a boy pulls off his shoes, his shirt, runs lazy eights of rain.

They wake in the dark, the heat of their sleep between them.
She swings her hips over his with the clatter of rain.

The road's a sudden river, trees thunder with dripping,
the sky no longer belongs to itself. All the world is rain.

A Roadside Diner in Iowa

Maybe you came here to read
the local news—obituary,

obituary, barn raising—but became
distracted by the boys playing Pac-Man

in the back hall with that reckless,
sixteen-year-old joy, and you

were a small boat drifting back
a muddy river of years. Or maybe

you have driven thousands of miles,
your father dead three states away,

but all you can think about is how
you'll never make love again

to that girl you knew in high school,
and you miss her small shoulders

and the way she smelled of apples,
so you order a slice of pie

and with that first hot forkful
you know, no matter what,

you can keep driving. Maybe
you come here every day,

because here every day is the same
and you love that above all things,

as your days are most times hard
and wrong and wrapping your cracked

hands around a cup of milky coffee
is the best thing you know.

Maybe you are poor but Vera keeps
the toast coming all afternoon.

Maybe you are not so poor.
Maybe the world is like that

and there is nothing you can do.
Maybe this is your life—

corned-beef sandwich, fries,
one thin, bright slice of orange.

Letter to Liz from Houston

You never see the sun in this city.
Gray sky always between you and light,
freeways like the wings of stone birds.
I walked north today, up old Delano Street, past
shotgun shacks and scrawny trees. Broken glass
ran the gutters like water. Liquor stores were legion.
This city's cut in half by color, and both sides
make my face Yankee so it won't fit. Grandmothers
watched me. They never smiled. Yesterday,
Quinton came to class with cigarette
burns all down his neck—ripples on the dark pond
of his body. The paper says the Guadeloupe River
is still bloated in the west. From every corner
of the Third Ward you can see Houston's square shoulders,
massive shadows grieving these streets. I walked back.
I miss you. (I think of the curve of your throat,
making these words.) On the way to work each day
I see a car wreck. The traffic, the stares—bloom
of red in gray. I have over a dozen kids
who are homeless—I teach them how to add integers
and after school they stand at Chapman and Providence,
shift on their feet as I drive away. Houston's grandmothers
see right through me. I'm trying to believe love
can be shadow and stone wing, a river of glass
over its banks and rising, still rising.

He is Only Six and Has Not Yet
Seen Anyone He Loves Die

The stars snap open like wet mouths,
      and the boy drapes a flannel jacket
across his father's shoulders and sits beside him
      on a three-legged camp stool
and rocks in slow circles; he hears
      the wooden knock of each leg on the earth
and the cries of coyotes like laughter,
      like little girls.

Yet his father calls the coyotes *Old dogs*,
      so when the boy hears it, a dark bell
of howl rung and rung, he just thinks
      It must be the oldest dog,
but then he sees his father has craned forward,
      his flannel and tin cup of whiskey forgotten,
his mouth slow and open, and the boy
      watches his father lip the word, *Wolf*.

Highway

The deer hide gloves slip from his hands,
                                    chafe his wrists,
fill with the scratch of alfalfa leaves. Beyond the field, the highway
glistens. The boy puts his shoulder to a bale
and heaves it over. Stunned mice

                              scatter. He turns,
sights down the neat line of bales the stacker
will soon jaw up. In the sky
                        the sun hangs. The field shakes
with heat. He walks and walks and under his boots he hears
the pop and snap of cut grass stems,

                              like the slender bones
he once found in a mudnest. His mother cries at the kitchen table.
The man who is not his father drives the stacker behind him.
The boy stops and stares past the fence—
                              at the highway,
where a diesel rig sings down the far hills. The sky is unbearably
white and wide, and the boy opens
                        his mouth and, for a moment,

that highway song is his.

A Dream of Home

In defense of whatever happens next
now the fields are thick with bluestem
and the river always runs
the wind still hauls dust but the boy
who called you weak buys you whiskey
and begs another story
your mother lies down
to love a man the Durango cactus on the sill
blooms and blooms things still bleed
but blood is good again
in the far field you see your father
so far away you run for him
he calls to you but oh
what's he saying

Mississippi Delta

If they ask what it was like, say green tangles of cypress steaming in the
    sun's white ache, say a one-eyed grandmother rocking on a rot-
    wood porch, say cotton stalks clacking in the dead of winter,
    dry as bones.

If they ask how it felt, say first the adventure of accent and miles of new
    road, then the fact of shotgun shacks and young girls dancing
    in dirt yards, say scarves of dust falling across their sun-dazzled
    shoulders, and say, finally, that rust-yellow dog with plum-size
    ticks studding his ears who sat beside your door waiting for
    dinner scraps and one day curled up by the pecan tree and
    died.

If they ask what you heard, say a bass note of bullfrog, of gunshot,
    of twelve-inch woofer blasts from the back of Elijah Love's
    Escalade. Say rivers were noiseless. Say the cicadas were like a
    scream. Say you never heard a train.

When they ask what people always ask, how was the food, just say pork
    butt and white bread, butter beans, stuffed catfish.

If they ask about thirst, go ahead and tell them old men buried their
    faces in the new graves of paper sacks, tell them boys sucked
    down cold cans of Mountain Dew just the same, tell them
    houses burned even though there's water,

but tell them too about the rain, how it came like a river and you woke
    to thunder and the whole wet world trembled and shone. And
    if they ask anything else, tell them about the day you left, the
    Arkansas bridge a lifetime of iron, the far hills and trees and in
    the rearview the sun rising—that reflection on your face, a fire.

The Evening Watering

Now the heat of the day has risen,
and the air, not so still, begins to breathe
in the silver rippling leaves of cottonwood
and that blushing mess of morning glories

she arcs the lip of her tin bucket towards
just as he reads the words—*at the breath
of God's mouth the waters flow*—and looks up
to see a river slip from her hands.

The Land to the North

After he died he got up and went north,
to the hills that curve with wind

before the land breaks
into tangles of rock near the Missouri.

This was a long way from where he had been,
from his house near town, his wife,

her trembling hands.
He had been there too long and was anxious to leave.

The land to the north was open wide as sky,
the wind blew in curves and circles.

These things were as he remembered.
And the sun, white as bone, reaching out, touching

everything. But many things were not
as he remembered.

Where were the trails he rode?
The creeks playing their stone and water songs?

Why these gray boards, falling?
He turned and went back. He found his bed empty,

his old wife curled on the couch with only
a thin blanket. Though he knew,

he lay down beside her as best he could.

Hallelujah, Somewhere, Steel

Drunk as all the drunk fathers,
holding their stools to the sawdust
floor of the Sportsman Bar with their sad
weight, we sang a fierce song of dirt
road hallelujah and getting out.

It was Justin, his hair long and holes
in his jeans, my younger brother, Paul,
and me. We spit rocks down Main Street
and dared the girls basketball team
with cheap amphetamines.

We weren't meant for this kind
of destruction—the way a wheat field
breaks in hail, the pure anger of Cathy Wilson
and the Congregational Church's Lady Republicans.
This place kept telling us we were wrong.

We knew somewhere
was a cool street, just dark, smoke
of a cigarette and a wild girl with her arms
around the man who was each of us.
She lipped the wild word *live* to our ears.

But we only had money for two six-
packs, a bottle of vodka, and enough gas
to rattle my father's farm truck down
a dozen knots of back road and up
to the high, dark plain of Rig Butte,

where the wind was hard,
the dry grass bent and cracked, and Justin climbed
the rig's black steel, black hammer pulling oil,
swinging him up and up in the black sky—and there
he let loose the steel and leapt for somewhere.

Meditation on the Treason of His Body

Bent over books of the economic
and social development of Latin America,
my brother is dying. I have only been once
to see him, there in the gray light rushing
like water down Arthur Avenue, over the black
wrapped heads of grandmothers moaning
prayers at the steps of Our Lady of Mercy,
down the throats and into the lungs of young
men bending against the black stones of Bronx
tenement houses. And there I saw his body
turned on itself, insurrection of MS—left eye
white and blinking, the hung flesh of his face,
bird's legs and trembling hands. He is 24.
He has gone gauzy in the light, his shadow
on the sidewalk only half as black as mine.
But in the evening, after we eat ravioli
from the market and share a quart of beer,
after he lays out a syringe and translucent
vial of oily medicine, scrubs his pearl belly
and slips the needle in, little red bulb of skin
in chemical blossom, he lets his shirt fall
across his still wide shoulders and opens
his book and studies.

Daybreak, Spokane, September 2001

They're tearing down the Olympia Beer sign
from atop the Empire Hotel.

The geese wing south again,

above the char color of the city,
through the still dark house of the sky.

Last week a woman threw herself in the river.

   * * *

I dream winter—wind leaning hard
down the mountains, blown snow

and ice—reading James Wright
for the first time.

How sad and lovely,

because in his poems everything and everyone
was always dying,

yet looking up from the page
I had never before wanted so wholly to live.

   * * *

Across the black river, I watch

bricks fall from the hotel without sound,
flowers of smoke blossom above the coal stacks,

and now the first sun break shivers me
in my dew-soaked shoes.

It is time to grieve, to believe in the world again.

Ruins

The white line unravels and I drive south
down Highway 51, a phantom road through levee
towns broke and open as half-hung
screen doors:
                    Wickliffe, Bardwell, Sassafrass Ridge—

here's the toothless maw of old downtown,
the bottle works a scrim of shattered glass,
                                        derelict
tracks that cut the place in half, muddy-footed boys
tossing rocks at stumps.

* * *

Last summer in Sunflower, Mississippi,
a black family rented a house across the tracks,
on the white side of town. My neighbors
said they were the first,
                    ever. Within a week
it burned to the foundation, the whole town
a hive of smoke.

* * *

I've been lost three times since Chicago, since 6 AM
and my first plate of buttered grits in months—

                                    the South
begins somewhere outside Ashley, Illinois, where that two-lane
landed me in a cotton field, a cypress swamp, now the ruins

of Hickman, Kentucky.

* * *

I teach 9th grade algebra in the little bayou town
of Indianola, Mississippi, and last year,
                            the one-hundred

and thirty-third since Mississippi sent Hiram Revels
to the US Senate, the thirty-ninth since Fannie Lou Hamer
told the Democratic National Convention she was beaten
unconscious on the dirt floor of the Indianola jail for trying
to register to vote, the ninth since the old-age death of the man
who hung a gin-fan around Emmet Till's neck and sunk him
in the Tallahatchie,
                        in the presidentiad of George W. Bush,
in the Year of our Lord 2003, out of the 156 children
that walked into my classroom every day, 154 were black—

all the white kids go to the academy across the tracks.

* * *

Long haulers truck loads of toaster ovens
bound for the great,
                      glistening acres of box-stores
that ring Cordova, Tennessee. Tourists who can't find

the freeway drive for all their worth to get out quick.
Near the Hickman Liquor Mart, old men lounge
on hunks of levee stone.
                      I drive right through
the guts of town, but they eye me still
with indifference.

* * *

It slides off your tongue like a goddamn snake—

Mississippi.

* * *

The ancient river people hauled reed buckets
of black mud for temples the river always

                                        washed away.

Only dirt mounds are left, sudden domes
of kudzu and blackberry

and the far highway carrying me south.

* * *

—n. *1. a cardinal point of the compass lying directly opposite*
north. 2. the direction in which this point lies.
                                        3. A region
or territory situated in this direction. 4. the general area south
of Pennsylvania and the Ohio River
and east of the Mississippi,
                                        consisting mainly
of those states that formed the Confederacy.

—adj. *5. lying toward or situated in the south;*
proceeding toward the south. 6. coming from the south,
as a wind.

           —adv. *7. to, toward, or in the south.*
8. into a state of serious decline, loss, or the like.

* * *

Once, on hall duty at Cassie Pennington Junior High,
I watched the school principal chase down a boy,
tackle him, and beat him with his fists.

The boy's name was Jermaine. He was fifteen
and read at a 2nd grade level. Two months later Jermaine
broke another boy's jaw.
                    That boy sat in the front row

of my 7th period class, his smooth face swollen and bent,
and refused to do his work.

* * *

But this morning

                    the half-light lit the fields
like fire—cotton bolls gone red and gold,
the paper leaves of corn, soybeans
shining with something deep inside.

                       And now,
as the sun escapes, the world goes water dark
and in the trees the soft slap of wind rises.

* * *

I'm less than six hours out. I'm going back to Mississippi
but I'm talking about America here—

                      the rot-wood
of The River Hotel in Cairo, shotgun shacks set back
in the trees,
          or a street in south Memphis, blue neon
hissing, rage of a cigarette, the warehouse door
banging on its hinge.

A Dream of Home

This time I'm ten years old
flipping my jackknife at the walls
sunburnt tired home from work
my mother clacks her teeth at what I've done
I run to the dark shed
sit in the straw by my dead
father's shit-stained boots
his feet fill the boots
he hauls a metal bucket loaded
with good grain he says nothing to me
only calls the sheep from the field

Bull Mountain Seasonal Bestiary

Summer Skunk

Driving fast down Ragged Point Road
in the old blue Ford, shadows eating

the day's last arc of color from the mountains—
I hit something. It could be somebody's dog,

so I grind to a stop but know soon enough—
my watery, stinging eyes, my mouth filled

with rancid butter—it's no dog. Only a small
bundle of darkness on the roadside, but what

a mountain of stink. Even the coyotes, fat
and yipping in the far fields, will taste this.

Fall Coyote

He's weak, my grandfather says, as he kneels
over the dead ewe—her stomach a great

dark cave, rump chewed and mangled.
An old kill. The pack must have moved on

without him, and he can't bring anything
down. Yet I still see long yellow teeth

and ask if we'll poison the carcass. *No,*
my grandfather says. *We'll let the old dog eat.*

Even calves are too big for him now.
Antelope too fast. He'll die come winter.

Winter Antelope

The first bullet breaks his shoulder—
in the scope I see his front leg hinge

with the wind and swing. The second
hits the heart and knocks him down.

Helluva shot, my grandfather growls,
as we kneel, the steaming curve of him

across the cold earth in front of us.
Maybe a last memory of leaping,

I think, as a meadowlark calls, as I
gut him with a bright, whetted knife.

Spring Meadowlark

Out north they sing in the summer:
Snow melt quickens Willow Creek,

the prairie goes bright as sky with grass,
and I see their burning yellow breasts—

little thumbs of color in the cottonwoods,
small suns that rise through shadow—

heave and fill and play the wide sky
with a sound like rain on stone and water,

and the skunk, his long sleep finally
broken, steps around a rotted stump.

A New Trembling

You know what it's like. The way
the fog closes the world behind you,
the gray smell of smoke through rain,
how the cracked boards of shacks curve
like scurvied bones. The sun grows
so terrible as it sets over the river.

But this day is a new trembling, a small
current across the waters. Nothing will die
on this day. For it was all pulled dripping
from the darkness only moments ago.

Mississippi Sonnet

When you drive to Jackson in the dark,
the highway's white as old bone. Far off lights
of cropper shacks float eternally away
from you, the incredible heaviness
of rivers. You swallow the damp smoke
of burnt chaff, houses, tree stumps.
Of course someone is waiting for you,
someone with dusky hair and cypress eyes.
What songs of sadness and old rivers
does she sing? Do you see yourself in her songs?
Are you there, in a field of wind,
your back bent to the earth? You drive to her
to keep this night from shattering,
like a dry bone, in your hands.

The Big Dry, Montana, 1985

Afternoon
Dust roostertails over the county road, blossoms like a dirt flower above the cottonwoods, rains down on our hands and faces as we splash through what's left of the river.

Thunderstorm
Grandma's hiding under the bed again. My brother and I run to the window: small fists of hail beat against the gravel, the wheat slowly folds on itself.

Wind
Pours down the far hills and across the prairie. Snaps the bunchgrass, fills the air with dust, the soap smell of sage.

Heat
In the dark I kick the sheets from the bed, splay my sweating arms and legs. Somewhere, a dog raises its snout to the moon and howls.

Coyote
There's another kill in the north pasture. I study the gnawed haunches, the empty cave of gut. The head and shoulders are untouched. I kneel, take the lamb's face in my hands.

Wind
Takes dew from the grass before anyone wakes.

Evening
I find an old length of 2x4 and step over the snare-caught rabbit. I steady, aim, and swing the board hard across its skull. It jumps and screams. I never knew rabbits could scream. I hit it again and again and through my tears don't notice when it goes limp.

Neighbor
They pull up a camper and move the oldest girl out there when the bedrooms fill up. Her face is a wide, white moon. Her hair straw. She's never been to school. I walk the county road to the river, and she watches me.

River
In the shallow, stagnant pools that are left, carp flap and suck for air. We wait until they're mostly dead, then wing rocks at them. A spray of dry, shining scales.

Church
I set the rabbit in an old cage out back to keep it from the dog. I wipe at my eyes and decide that if I can wash the blood out I'll skin it tomorrow and make a gift of the hide to the dark-haired girl who sits in the pew in front of us.

Wind
Father comes in from a day on the tractor, his neck and face blown raw. Mother lays him down on the couch and rubs wool-wax into his skin. My brother and I watch from the across the room. She sings softly. She is so tender with him. He smiles up at her. For a moment they have forgotten us, and everything else.

Night
Bright clot of stars in the bowl of sky.

Heat
Grandma hands me an ice cube to run over my forehead, my lips. She says she's never seen it like this before. She pauses, says it again.

Coyote
Father brings three of them home in the bed of the truck. My brother and I climb the wheel wells and dare each other to touch their tails, their claws, their yellow eyes.

Wind   '
The mountain's on fire, the sun just a bright stone in a river of rippling smoke. I breathe ash.

Thunderstorm
I wing my shirt over my head and run naked circles in the gravel. I open my bird's mouth wide to the sky. It's not much, but rain enough to cool the evening and wet the dust.

Neighbor
She slaps him hard on the head. She yells some more and grabs him and turns him around and kicks him in the butt. He falls down the porch steps, and I flinch. She looks at me, asks if I want some too. I say, *No.*

Church
We're always the last to leave. We always have everything to pray for.

River
It's just not there anymore.

Morning
I spit on the whetstone like my father taught me and sharpen a slender blade. But when I go out back, the rabbit's alive, hopping slowly around the cage, its fur matted with dirt and blood.

North Carolina by Greyhound:
First Christmas After the Funeral

1.

The bearded man in Rapid City
wears a dress, and I sleep
through Minneapolis. In the backseat
a boy just older than me
slips his hand under the sequined shirt
of a girl laid out across his lap. He reaches
her left breast and works it
slowly, like dough. When we stop
at Bluefield, the bus driver gives me
thirty-cents to buy
a bag of chips. And in the neon dark
Chicago is the smell of burnt skin.

2.

My life is in this bus—
mother, sister and brother,

some stories about a father
and the South. There's three years

of ragged comics
in my suitcase, and I've written

all the letters to Grandma
I can write. *Soon,*

my mother says, *we'll see
where he was born.* But the sign

says *Ohio,* the highway's lost
to rain, and the hiss

and flare of cigarettes
has me coughing.

3.

Wheeling, West Virginia, is a tongue of dirty river
licking at its banks, brick stacks
breathing fire, and a man—
whose skin I've heard of but never seen—
black as three-day coffee. The bathrooms
at the station cost a nickel
but some church has pie
for free. Fancy Gap stinks of rotting leaves
and gasoline. I count stops
at night by marking on my arms.
In the daylight I can't see anything
for all the trees.

4.

My mother's hands shake
against the glass. *Look*,

she whispers, *this
is Carolina*, her face so slick

with tears I can taste
the salt. I close

my eyes. I'm tired
of looking out the window,

of cheese sandwiches
and tap water, of all the tangled

stories. It doesn't matter—
he's not here either,

and I don't even
remember his face.

Letter to Paul from Sunflower

It's hot here. The air is heavy.
August has been a long scream of cicadas.
The Big Sunflower River runs swollen
and brown. In a whisper of wet fog, blackbirds
spray from my pickup, and off old Highway 49
rice and cotton give way to strangles of trees
along the bayous. They say the topsoil is hundreds
of feet thick—the rot of a continent washed over
and over again. Even the sun, just a gray ring
in grayer sky, is choked in it all. And yesterday
I saw a thousand white cranes smother
a stand of dying cypress like snow.

I stay in a small brick house on the white
side of Sunflower. My neighbors smile,
bring me big plates of okra casserole
and invitations to drink sweet tea on their porch.
I smile back, thank them for their hospitality,
and walk across the tracks, to the school
where I teach. My students are kids like any others,
but they're also poor and black and beaten
down every day by the blows of the dead,
and of the living. I like to think I'm doing
something about this, but then I cash my check
and make my way home, again across the tracks.

You can buy a watermelon at Lewis's Grocery
for a dollar. The big woman says, *Now, you pick
you a sweet one. If it ain't sweet, you bring it back
and get you a sweet one, you hear?* I pick
a sweet one. Children clatter across the slumped
porches of shotgun shacks. The men down
King Avenue hold paper bags close to their hearts
and stare. There's a grandmother with one eye
who talks to stray dogs—this place is deep
with ghosts. Do you remember that Sunday,
driving Montana? Just the two of us, tall grass
and sky? Brother, you are far away,
and America is so suddenly old.

Turning

My brother and I sat on either end of the plow,
levering our small weight down to the blades
sunk neck deep in dirt. We watched the things
of the field break against steel—grouse eggs
and rocks, tangles of snake, old cow bones,
vines of wild plum, chokecherry, and rose.

The tractor breathed hard and black, the lynch pin
howled a metal howl, and the plow blades bit down
to earth, rock, and root. Over the scream of it,
we heard nothing our father said. My brother pointed
to him, his lips moving with mute breath. Soon,
though we knew he still sat in the scoop seat

of the tractor, we could not see him, as he was lost
in a flickered drift of heat and dust. We were all
a slow blooming swath of black around green—turning,
and again turning, I rode that steel knowing
we would finally turn into ourselves. When the sun
swung to the farthest pale of the sky, father cut

the choke, and the tractor shrieked to a stop.
We fluttered from our plow perches and played
at his heels all the way to the house. The day
was young, and we were young and did not mind
the broken land, ghost of the engine still grinding
in our ears. After lunch, he slumped in the brown-

hatched easy chair as our mother worked
his shoulders. Noses pressed to the rainbow ink
of last Sunday's comics, we did not see the ragged
catch in the piston of his chest or feel the rock-caught
tremble that ran the length of him. That day we turned
the last green over, and, months later,

thrashing through the white sheets of his hospital bed,
cursing our childish noise because he was delirious
with a turning pain that bit clear down to his bones, he kept
asking mother how much was left to plow, if the tractor
was full of diesel, if maybe he shouldn't finish it tomorrow—
or if the wild plum was too thick, and the rose.

A Dream of Home

For this I will need a claw hammer
a rust-gutted Chevy Luv six miles of fence sloped
and broken as an old man's smile
and give me too the old man
say my dead grandfather my dead father
it doesn't matter just a strong back
and a face that knows the dirt sorrow
and dirt grace and good dust of dead things
the way we race and clatter across the prairie
breathing from beneath the Luv's tires dust
breathing the whole sweet world breathing us

The Log Works Near Midnight

I've left the house of the famous poet,
where we ate moose and salmon, mused
of coyote snares, welding, and the sad

death of small towns—and now,
near midnight, wreaths of fog round
the meadows, hills soaked in strange

pools of moonlight, I'm just drunk
and tired of pretending I live life timed
to the curve of the sun, pulse hot

for spare dollars. My barrel-chested father
is dead these fifteen years, I sit and write,
and those four men, gliding through

the gloom light of the log works,
turn to leave the long day. Overhead,
the beautiful and useless stars wheel.

Trying to Find Hollandale, Mississippi

Morning

I make my way through the fog, slowly.
A diesel truck slips by with wild
lights. The highway
reveals itself, moment
by moment. Each bend and curve a necessary
birth, some child of disaster. Crows
peel dark wings from the sky.
The cypress trees reach out,
then away. There is much here
I do not see.

Late Afternoon

Now they're burning cotton fields.
I pull over, watch fire's ragged breath
calm to acres of ash.
The wind picks up,
and suddenly the sky has no choice
but to begin a new life—
dark against washed miles of light.

Sunset

I kneel in river mud, hold
a wet stone close
to my chest. Across the water,
the sunlit eyes
of a stray dog blaze up
in the darkening sky. An owl calls.
I have no idea where I am.

Houston Sonnet

Years ago I was lost for an entire summer
in Houston. I couldn't find my way
from Delano Street, did not believe there was a door
that led out of Enrique's Pool Hall, or any path
from the cracked lip of that cup of warm beer.
I was trying to be a good junior high math teacher
but was sick in the heart, that poor burbling
organ, meaty thwack and flush of blood—it was all
too hot, and when the air-conditioner
in my classroom broke, I opened the windows,
and we all wheezed and coughed smoke,
the Third Ward up in flames,
and Quinton raised his hand and asked,
Why do cities burn so easy?

Memphis Closes Her Eyes

Friday, and I need a drink. Something strong
because it's rice harvest, so much dust, steel,
and sun. A boy throws sticks to a dog twisting
in the street. I'm working too damn hard.

Mr. Lake, my next door neighbor, an easy hundred,
oldest of seven dead brothers, trembles to stand
like grass in the wind, is waiting in my driveway
to tell me Johnny Cash, like each of his brothers,

is dead. So I drive to Memphis. Let bourbon
roar down my throat. Watch chaff fires burn
like gods as the sun goes down. Then I'm walking
Union Avenue—drunks and lunatics and bits

of paper drift across the street. A man holds
a cigarette to his lips. Blue neon lights in the gray
of his eyes—and I know there is a song for all of this,
something hard and wild, black as night, and rising.

The Bone Yard: A Phone Conversation with My Brother

Here is the old ram, a winter dead,
        the dark swirl of empty
socket and splintered nose,
        teeth wide as thumbs, scaly
horns that swing around. We crack
        the jawbone from its greasy
hinge, pack the brain pit
        with dirt and send it
winging against a tree.
        And now my brother,
who is younger than me
        and moved to the city,
says, Remember the flies, and I see them:
        On the just dead and dumped
they are a new skin—
        iridescent, dark, and loud.
Not even a handful of slung
        gravel scares them
from the rot. So we wait,
        let the flies do the first work
and then sun and wind, rain,
        and sun again—
and now we come, walking the north road
        to the bone yard,
our old dog chasing sparrows.
        We lean the long leg bones
against the ditch bank,
        break them with our boots,
then bring the marrowed hollow,
        still wet, to our noses—
smell the sweet mystery
        of blood. Like our father,
dead these twenty years,
        a man neither of us knew.
My brother brings him up,
        not much, just an image
he takes as memory—
        dark hair, chaff and sweat,

cheeks black with tractor grease,
              that same old collie dog.
But it is enough. And now, finally,
            we begin: From the field, we pack
his bones, sun-dried and gleaming,
           crack them on our knees.

Somewhere South of Miles City

Stop the car. There. Now
breathe with me. That broken

Ford needs only a swift kick
to set it right. Listen. The radio

man says *For Sale*, says *Believe*.
You believed in me. I believed

in highways. We fell in love.
I'm sorry. I know this bone-white

sky isn't right. I had to see it
myself. Stare down the throat

of a double-wide, walk the blasted
streets of Billings. This was me,

years before you. I wanted to say
Montana again, and mean it.

Yes. I know. It's never enough.
The world is mostly broken.

But listen. Breathe with me.
Taste the dust. We have

three days of highway. I'll drive,
carry these nowhere bones. Home.

Killing the Murnion Dogs

I.

The moon rose wide and red over the gravel
bed of the river as Willie Murnion's dogs slipped

across Highway 12 and ran the flat miles
north through sage and greasewood—

seven slick little cow dogs and that night
they were all fast and wild, their jaws clicking

with spit and dust and the bright daub
of blood that is the full moon.

II.

That morning I remember magpies
wheeling overhead,

dark in the pale sky
and screaming

for a meal. And the lambs—
broke clean in half, sheep torn open

at the belly, gray loops
of entrails soft

in the sun. Some were still
alive, bleating heavy.

I was only six
but had learned to count.

There were thirty ewes.
I lost track of all the lambs.

III.

Though we drove north together,
father and son, to fix fence

and eat cheese sandwiches at noon,
I don't remember him at all.

I don't know if he swore,
if he told me to hide my eyes,

if he knelt in the tall grass
and cried. In my memory,

he is gone and I am alone
in the cab of the old green Ford

and there are ripped bundles
of wool and blood

and dark birds, and this is bad
because the river has run dry

and even in my child's mind
I know this means we might lose

the ranch. The sun rises and the sky
is the blue of ice, then the blue of water.

IV.

Days later there were the pictures
in the county paper—

my mother pointing at the torn
and bloated carcasses,

my father and Willie Murnion
staring at their boots,

and one of me,
my small hand wrapped

around the spiral horn
of a fly-bitten skull.

V.

My father's lying on a white bed in the hospital in Billings, his skin
a chemical yellow, a halo of black curls around his rapidly balding
head. Three years ago the Murnion dogs slaughtered our sheep, and
I am nine now and standing quietly by the side of the bed and
the nurses are talking about bone marrow and lymph nodes—and I
don't understand anything.

He dies in February. Snow, funeral: my mother with her arms
across her chest, the priest singing, and all these strong men gone
weak with tears, crescent moons of tractor grease beneath their
fingernails, patting me on the back, telling me I'm the man of the
house now, man house now. I remember this, and the hospital—but
I don't remember anything else. To this day I don't remember my
father outside of sickness and death.

The drought hit hard that summer. My mother cried each week at
Sunday Mass and took a part-time job at the county school to make
ends meet. I got a new pair of work jeans for my tenth birthday and
started irrigating the whole place in June. I'd wake in the hot night,
the rasp of locusts hard and loud, pull on my rubber hip-boots, kick
the dirt bike into gear, and haul-ass out to the field to slop around
for hours in moonlight and mud. I messed up a lot, and foxtail,
which even sheep won't eat, bloomed along the ditches.

But we made it. By some grace we kept the ranch, and though I
wasn't aware of it at the time, my father slipped from memory. He

was something I knew about but didn't really know, like the summer rain the old men remembered. I have been told I helped him in the machine shed, fetching tools as he worked on the combine. And truly, I can feel the smooth steel of the wrenches, but I can't see the sweat that must have run down his sun-dark skin. There is the framed picture my mother keeps on the old piano top, the one of my father and the tamed magpie: He smiles and his sideburns are thick and the dark bird rests on his wrist. Even now I can hear it call with hunger, but in my mind the bird just caws and caws and my father never tosses it that fistful of stale bread. I remember the bloody mess of wool and meat, but I don't remember him.

A few years ago, at my uncle's house, we all watched some old home videos dug out of a basement closet. It was mostly shots of cousins as crawling babies and aunts as slender, long-haired mothers. But then, for a few seconds, he is there, leaning into the door frame, his shoulders like a hunk of board, his thick hair blue-black. I don't know this man. He tips his cap back on his head—and is gone.

VI.

Years later my mother tells me
the story of that day. She says

my father walks the dying
with his rifle, says he ends it

with a bullet in the ear.
Then turns us around, drives

fast down Highway 12,
and fast down Murnion Road.

And the dogs are just sitting there,
happy with dust and dried

blood on their champing jaws.
They play with me

like any old cow dogs,
while my father and Willie cut

seven lengths of rope. It's hot—
the dogs panting, now tied

to a cottonwood, sitting
on their bloody haunches in a ring

of dust where the river
should have been. My mother shudders

as the rifle fires and six dogs howl
for the one who is dead.

VII.

Magpies pick most bones clean
and the river still runs hard

from the mountains in the spring.
Our fields are full of foxtail and pine.

My father is everywhere
but memory: He rises with the moon,

his arms the gnarled stalks of greasewood,
his breath the hot wind on the plains.

He is river dust and sheep's blood
and any sky from ice to water.

A Dream of Home

I wake in the dark and remember
someone with their back to me
beneath a cottonwood
a barrel of rainwater and the wind
dust and dry grass in the wind

My wife a soft hill of sheets beside me
I rise and stand before the open window
somewhere in the night
a man says goddamn and laughs
a streetlight whines snaps off

This is the dark world I can do nothing
about but settle back
into darkness I wake in the dark
and remember

The Stone Eater

She does not understand how the time just after
her husband died, when she'd walk
crying for hours along the creek bank,
was so good.
            It's true she is alone and the fields
are fallow still, the blown dust of them
in her eyes most of the time. But this spring
the creek ran deep in its rocky bed,
and a cool wind licked the whole length of her
and the valley. Now, in the evenings, as one
the antelope rise on willow-thin limbs
and delicately lip the tall grass. And soon,
the strong young man who is her neighbor
will climb into his tractor for the harvest,
and the sun will be where it should in the sky
and the moon in the night and the mouths of stars
opening and opening: Her heart
and the world have found this usual way
to go on.
            Yet to remember the good pain
of her long ago walks, she pulls a cold,
broken stone from the bottom of the creek
and sets it beneath the warmth of her tongue.

Body Theology

The Gospel of Mark has its resurrection,
just like all the rest—
rich man's tomb thrown

open, white shroud
rumpled in the rocky corner. And where
is the beloved

body? Before they closed
the casket, my grandmother took
her husband's head

in her hands and worked the skin of his face
with her thumbs. Each spring,
she plants sage

on his grave, just to drop
to her knees and run her hands
through the earth.

At least Mark has the ending right—
the women came
to wash him, to touch him

one more time but he was
resurrected, gone, and they ran
and told no one.

The Schoolteacher Blues Again

Sunflower, Mississippi, 2002

The slump-backed fish cutters sluicing their blood hand, then their knife hand, out back of the plant in a ditch that drains to an acre trough lip full of a day's guts; Mr. Carver, one-time freedom rider and first black lawyer in town, shutting down his office on the second floor of the Planter's Bank building at the corner of Lee and Evers; the way the long fields back of Sunflower pulse like veins as the sun goes down; my neighbor telling me she wants her kids to *be with their own race, it's better that way*; her small daughter, all blonde hair and smiles, peeking at me from behind the bars of her mother's legs; the new place across town where tourists clap like idiots for mumbling, drunk Cadillac Jackson who swallowed half his teeth one morning when he woke to a tire iron across his face; a white rain of dogwood blossoms on the trim lawns of the big houses by the river; the men on buckets and cypress stumps staring through the smoke of their cigarettes and a blood sun as Mr. Carver makes his way across the cotton-run tracks, down Church Street, past old Freedom Hall and Junior's Joint, dogs pissing on piles of tumbled bricks; the music teacher down the hall whupping hell out of Orlando because too many of the words he knows are some derivative of mother-fucker; the private academy across town spit-shined to a gleam; the man who owns Sunflower Food Store helping my wife to her car, telling her *Yeah, maybe it'd be nice if they could all go to school together*, then just stopping, grocery bags in his hands; the girl in my 4th period class whose mother left for Memphis three weeks ago and hasn't come back; the house fires that flap and rage like bright hearts in the night; Mrs. Butler, who's pulled thirty-odd years of mop water across these floors, shuffling into my room, asking, *What'd you teach those children today, Mr. Wilkins?*

Shooting Carp

Noon sun was a white hole in the sky,
and I was the lovely

killer on the bridge. The river
nearly dry, smell of dirt

and sage, chokecherries stinking
on the branch. Childhood

is always too much,
or not enough. The old horror

that comes to nothing: dark
circle of grass beneath a cottonwood,

green bean casserole,
mother weeping in the barn. Anyway,

I drew a bead on a fat one,
tail swinging wildly in a splash

of mud and sunlight. We must
remember. To be forgiven

we must fill our lungs with cordite
and iron, see the waters

roll with blood.

The Names

It is no good to grow up hating the rich.
                    –B.H. Fairchild

That boy with nine fingers was beaten mean—
now his wheatshock hair is always flame.
The woman from Yellow Horse? Her second daughter
froze to death in a ditch. And Pete, did you know
that slender boy who in the fifth grade snuck a pack

of his father's Camels onto the recess yard?
Remember how we spat and choked and loved
every red-eyed minute of it? Near ten years ago,
laid off and drunk in this blasted land
of Reagan bankruptcy and corporate farming,

he took his little rust and yellow Chevy Luv
fishtailing down the gravel road out of Ingomar
and fast over Highway 12 where a trucker making time
hit him broadside at eighty. But you
know this. You've made your wise peace,

and though I've got no right, I somehow
don't care. Why not hate the rich? It's easy,
and some days easy's what I need. I lie down
in the spring wet alfalfa and hear the wind like water,
but then, always, the unraveling

clouds shift the sky into blue highway,
and the Newman boy guns his truck of dark cloud across it,
and when I open my eyes everything
is shattered. This country I call home is, like yours,
lost, and my people too are lost, like me,

so let me hate with them, let me sit up at the bar,
and curse the banker, the goddamn-silly-designer chaps
the new boss man from back east wears, let me speak
the names of the dead and get righteous,
for at least one more round.

Spiritual

Call this day necessary: No, call it sacrament—
the slow walk to Beards Hollow,
wind that cools our sun-washed faces,
spray of river and the river running out
to sea. Those birds, I know, were sent by God,
even though by *God* I don't know
what I mean. I mean, maybe we can blame
this blessing on right choices, lives lived mostly
well—the dog who loves us, those few good
friends, our happy tragedy of ordinary
lovers. But even in this joy I know enough
of pain and shame to say that's all wrong: No one
deserves this world. The old degraded
fisherman—his good nets eaten by the turtles,
the fish always flat and stinking, that one
mean as spit to children—he may beat us yet
to heaven. So I call it spiritual when seabirds
fill the sky with wings, and you claim
beach grass dances with the water but water
chooses sky. The hollow smells of wood
and tar, the rocks a shrine of barnacles and salt—
no matter the reason, it is given: This wind,
the way you laugh your dark eyes closed.

A Prayer

For girls—blue jeans, sunburn, acres of baked dust and cattle—
even now ass-down on the ground   even now making
a home of it: of weeds and bits of driftwood   of filthy
crescent moons beneath fingernails   elbow-crooks   winked-eyes:
Daddy home—tobacco spit, brass shells—to swing them sick
in the hot sky:
                          Even now running three times around
the double wide—*loves me   loves me   cow patty   not.*
For girls: hips wide as pickup seats   who O their mouths
for lipstick   cigarettes: drag main all day and who the fuck
cares: this is nowhere
                                    anywhere else is somewhere: Oh
now there are acres of baked dust and cattle: And skin
skin of boys   sun-dark   gleaming: Oh to peel their jeans
off them   love them   like coming   home: Oh those boys
stink like cowshit and talk worse   and who the fuck cares:
this is sunburn, nowhere, lipstick, and dust.

For those women with flour and lard for mouths, mouths
of dry sticks   rainbow   brass shells   rust: Now
they pitch coffee dregs out the screen door, pin a rock
on the tomcat's nose   ass-end   milked-eye:
                                              And this
man of hers, always lost in acres of baked dust and cattle,
always off and gone: lonesome O of her mouth rattling
with rotten teeth and interrogations: Who's to say
this is the half-of-it   the home-of-it   but who the fuck
can do anything about it?
                          For these women   nailing
themselves to the rough-cut boards   of their husbands: A man's
splintered   face gone   berserk with tears   dreams of fat cattle
tall grass   rain to crush the goddamn dust: For these women
with rainbows in their broken mouths.

For men—cowshit boots, tobacco breath, beercan eyes—
dead drunk and out cold on their bellies   in the woodshed
on the pool table at the Snake Pit   held in the white arms
of a raging wife: You see they just can't beat

this bad land
right: their cattle sacks of bone and dust   the river dust   sky
a scoured breath of dust: They get up   they sink
the plow in the belly of the blown earth   they put a bullet
in the steer's ear   they keep trying   they keep dying:
And again, again they water the sodding garden of themselves
with liquor:

knurled potato skin   onion eyes   turnip lips
morning glory for a tongue. For these men grown rank, wild:
These men like weeds   like boys loving   everything
too hard   and too much.

For boys who jack the truck up to eighty and slip
a hot hand up her skirt   play Waylon and take it
so goddamn seriously   smoke driftwood   slather
ranch dressing on everything   buck and jump
and believe—

Oh   daddy's a good man   I'm better
my fields will get green   my cattle fat   my best girl
will never eye the new schoolteacher twice—

who find a new
bright world in a beer can, who know better but shoot out
the streetlights anyway, who come   home and kiss their mothers
and fall dead   asleep in a tangle of flannel sheets and starlight.
For boys still ass-down in the sandbox,

building worlds—
Oh   fireweeds my fences   chips of driftwood my slow
grazing cattle—just like their only world—*Oh   this dust*
here is the good north pasture   and this dust here is home.

Notes

While real events, situations, and people have been referenced herein, it should be noted that this manuscript is a work of the imagination.

The italicized section in "The Evening Watering" is from Kathleen Norris's *Dakota*.

"Meditation on the Treason of His Body" is for Paul.

The definition included in the poem "Ruins" is from Random House's 1996 edition of *Webster's College Dictionary*.

"A New Trembling" is for Siena.

The poems of James Dickey, B. H. Fairchild, James Galvin, Richard Hugo, W. S. Merwin, Patrick Phillips, Barbara Ras, James Wright, and Kevin Young were essential in the drafting of this volume.

Joe Wilkins was born and raised north of the Bull
Mountains of eastern Montana. After graduating
from college, he spent two years teaching in
the public schools of the Mississippi Delta with
Teach For America. He is the author of a memoir,
The Mountain and the Fathers, and a previous
chapbook of poems, *Ragged Point Road*; his poems,
essays, and stories appear in the *Georgia Review*,
the Southern Review, *Harvard Review*, *the Sun*,
Orion, and *Slate*. He lives with his wife, son, and
daughter in north Iowa, where he teaches writing
at Waldorf College.